Classical Sheet Music For Solo Violin

Bach Sonatas and Partitas,
Nicolo Pagaini Caprices,
Rodolphe Kreutzer Etudes,
Pierre Rode Caprices,
Pietro Rivelli Caprices,
& Additional Selections

(114 Pieces in Total)

Compiled by,

Emily Rose

Fairhaven Press inc.

www.fairhavenpress.com

1

Classical Sheet Music For Solo Violin

Table of Contents

2

INTRODUCTION

THESE PIECES ARE CLASSIC SOLO VIOLIN PIECES OFFERED FOR AN INTERMEDIATE TO ADVANCED VIOLIN CLASS. THEY ARE COMMON PIECES OF CLASSICAL MUSIC USED FOR GENERATIONS TO ADVANCING VIOLIN STUDENTS. THERE ARE 110 SOLO PIECES AND FOUR MISCELLANEOUS SELECTIONS.

THE BACH SONATAS AND PARTITAS WERE WRITTEN IN THE EARLY 1700S DURING THE BAROQUE ERA. THEY CERTAINLY AREN'T EASY FOR LESS EXPERIENCED VIOLINISTS AND THE CHACONNE IN PARTICULAR CAN CHALLENGE EVEN THE MORE EXPERIENCED MUSICIANS.

NICOLO PAGAINI CAPRICES ARE GOOD FOR ADVANCING STUDENTS IN THAT EACH ONE FOCUSES ON A PARTICULAR AND DIFFERENT SKILL SET THAN THE OTHERS.

RODOLPHE KREUTZER ETUDES, WRITTEN IN THE LATE 1700S, ARE FUNDAMENTALS IN THE STUDY OF VIOLIN.

THE PIERRE RODE CAPRICES WERE COMPOSED IN THE 1800S AND HAVE BECOME A CLASSIC FOR VIOLIN STUDENTS. EACH IS IN A DIFFERENT KEY AND HELP THE STUDENT WORK ON THE BASICS.

THE 12 CAPRICES FROM PIETRO ROVELLI (1820S) COMPLETE OUR TRAINING PROGRAM WITH ADDITIONAL PRACTICE LESSONS.

THE REMAINING PIECES WERE CHOSEN BECAUSE OF PERSONAL INTEREST AMONG INSTRUCTORS AND STUDENTS.

-- EMILY

Sonata I

Adagio
(Signature retained in accordance with the original edition)

Fuga
Moderato

7

10

Sonata II

Edited by Leopold Auer
JOHANN SEBASTIAN BACH

11

Double
Allegro

13

14

Tempo di Bourrée

Double

I^{ma} volta f e detaché

II^{da} volta p e spiccato

Z

I.

II.

Aa

Bb

Cc

*) Middle of the Bow

* *II^{da} volta detaché - e - ritenuto*

Sonata III

Edited by Leopold Auer
JOHANN SEBASTIAN BACH

Grave
Lento

Fuga

Moderato assai

22

23

24

Sonata IV

Edited by Leopold Auer

JOHANN SEBASTIAN BACH

Allemande
Andante

Corrente

Allegro moderato

26

27

★) In some editions :-

Ciaccona

29

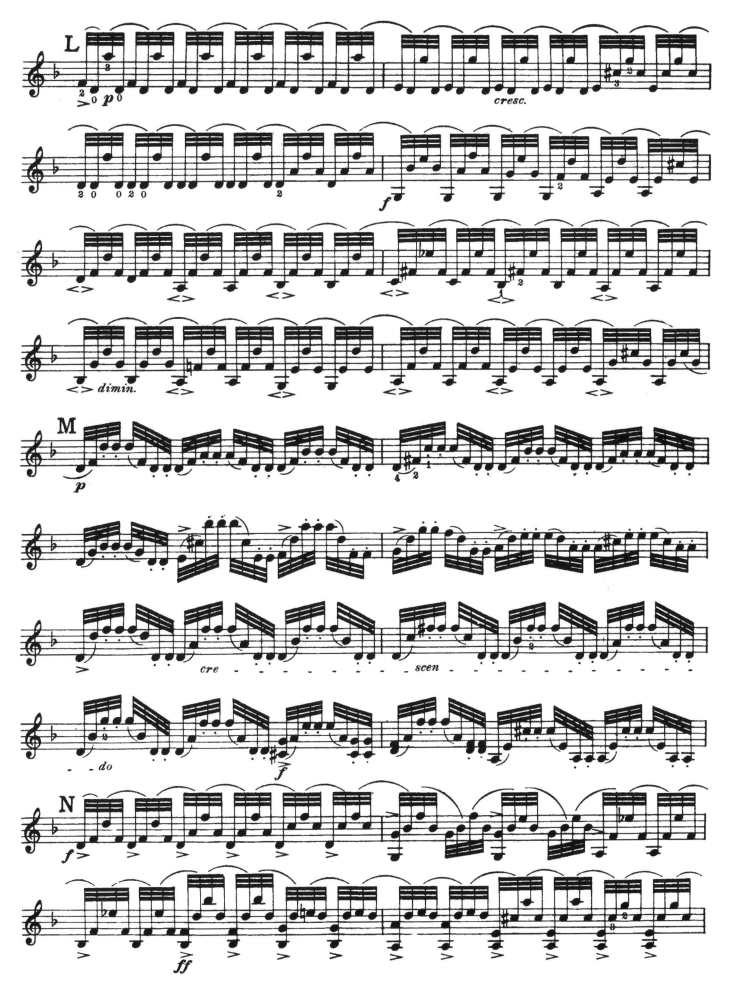

33

Sonata V

Edited by Leopold Auer
JOHANN SEBASTIAN BACH

*) In some edition:-

Fuga

Molto moderato

39

40

42

Sonata VI

Edited by Leopold Auer
JOHANN SEBASTIAN BACH

Preludio

44

45

Gavotte and Rondo

Menuetto I.

Menuetto II.

47

CHACONNE

Andante

J. S. BACH

49

50

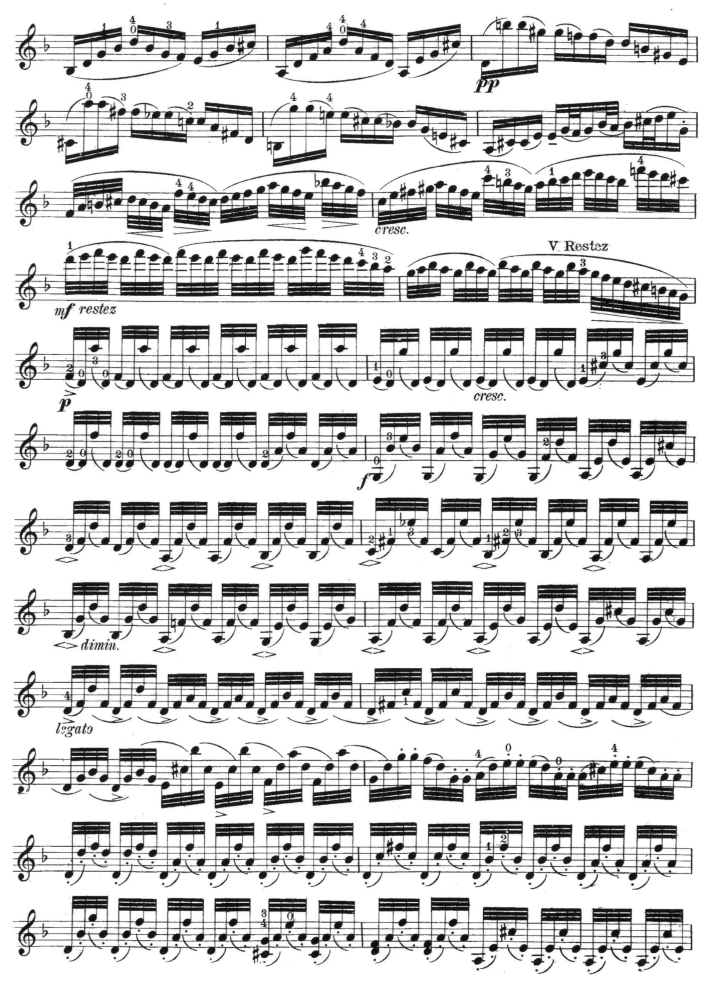

53

54

56

Air

by

Johann Sebastian Bach.

Violin.

Arr. by AUGUST WILHELMJ.

In order to produce every note distinctly and with brilliant clearness, the four notes of each arpeggio must be taken simultaneously and held for the duration of each chord combination. For effective rendition and mastery of spring-bow arpeggios and similar styles of bowing, see my Violin School, Part II (Virtuoso Technics.)

The double-stop passages in thirds with lightly thrown bow at the middle.

With light, rebounding bow, at the middle, through use of wrist only and absolutely without any assistance from upper arm. Special attention necessary for clear tone production in string transfers.

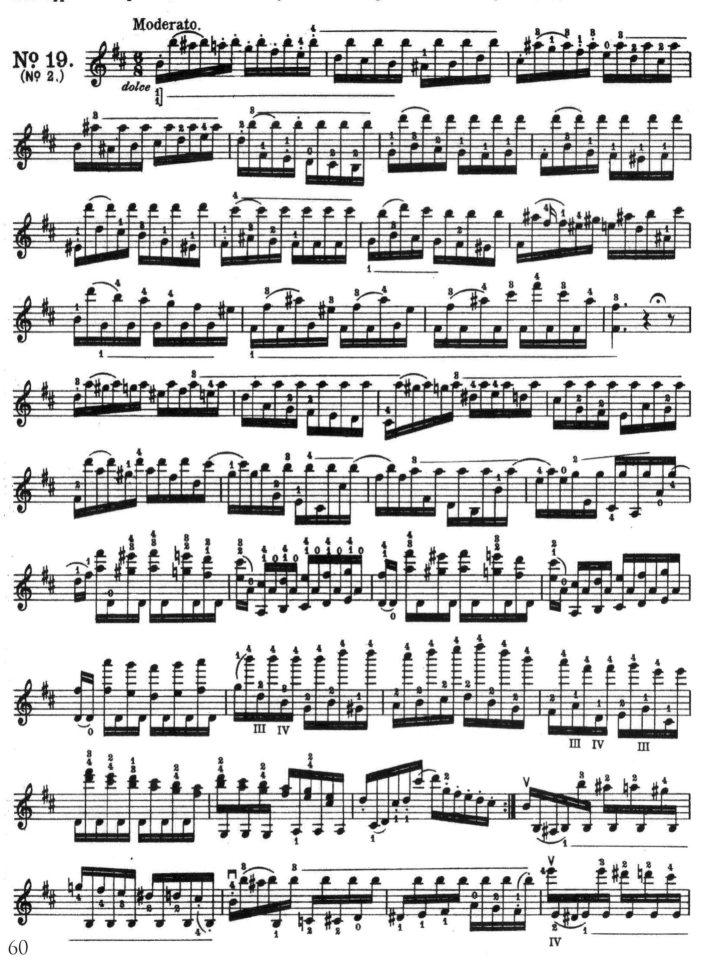

60

61

For preparatory or additional material for octave playing with fingering as used in this Caprice, see Part II of my "Violin School" and Book III of my "Systematic Scale Studies" (Carl Fischer, New York.)

The trills in this Caprice without after-beats.

Sostenuto.

Particular attention is necessary in this *Presto* to attain perfection in *Legato* playing.

Presto.

The suggestions for playing three-part chords as offered on page 5 (Caprice No. 3) also apply to the follow-
-ing Caprice. The bow is not to leave the strings and particular attention as to clearness and purity of intonation is necessary.

65

For suitable preparatory studies for the following Caprice, see my Violin Method, Part II, Virtuoso-Technics, as well as my "Systematic Scale Studies" Book II, Scales throughout four octaves.

N⁰ 2.
(N⁰ 5.)

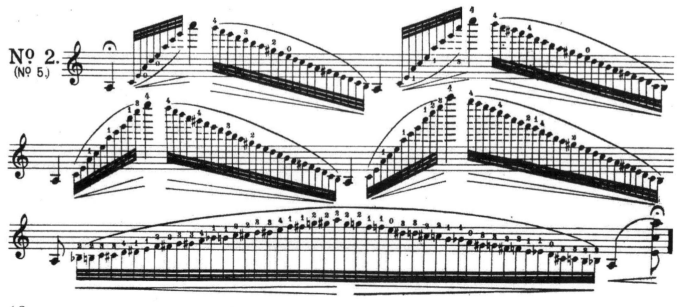

Up-and down-bow Thrown Staccato.

Agitato.

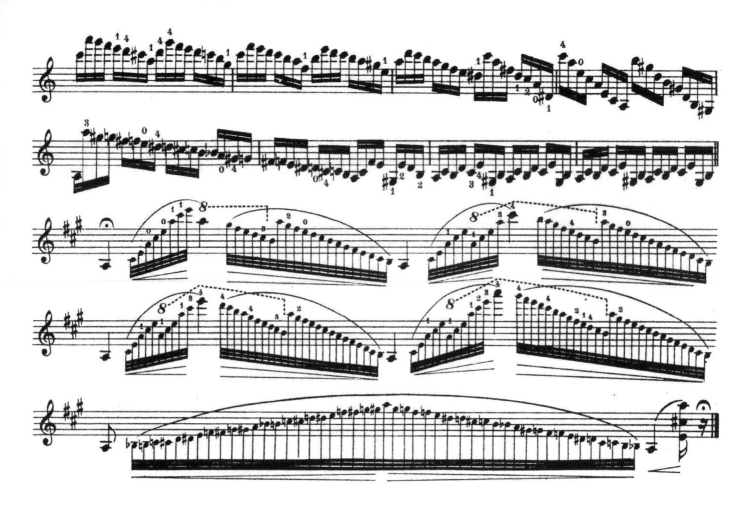

30

This Caprice, which is to be used for daily study, is of particular value for developing the strength, technical facility, stretching abilities and independence of the fingers.

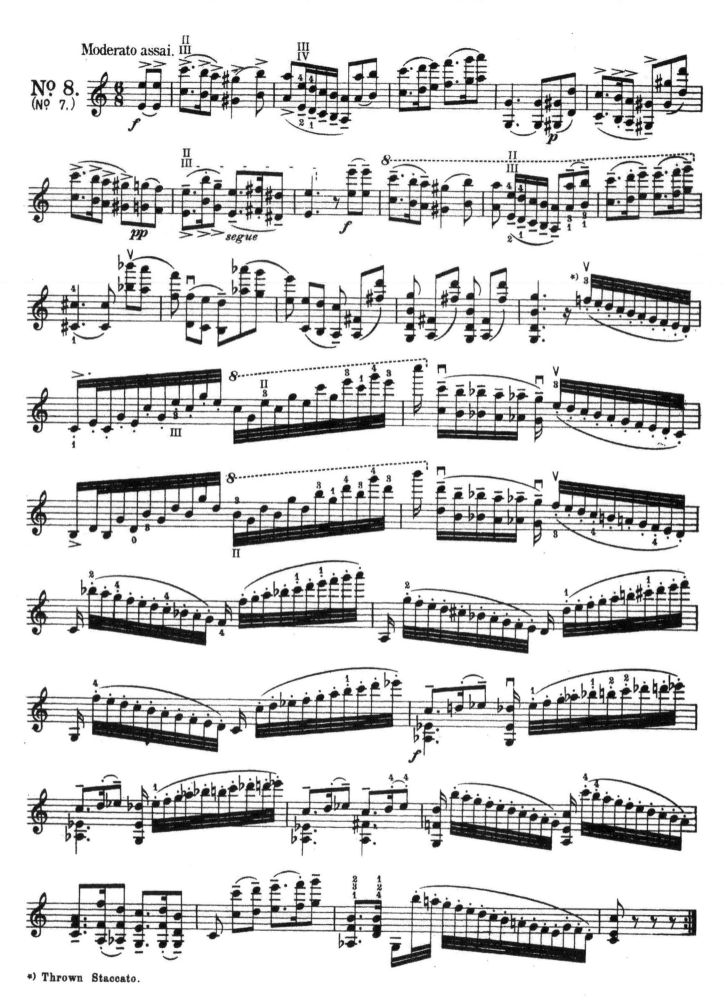

*) Thrown Staccato.

72

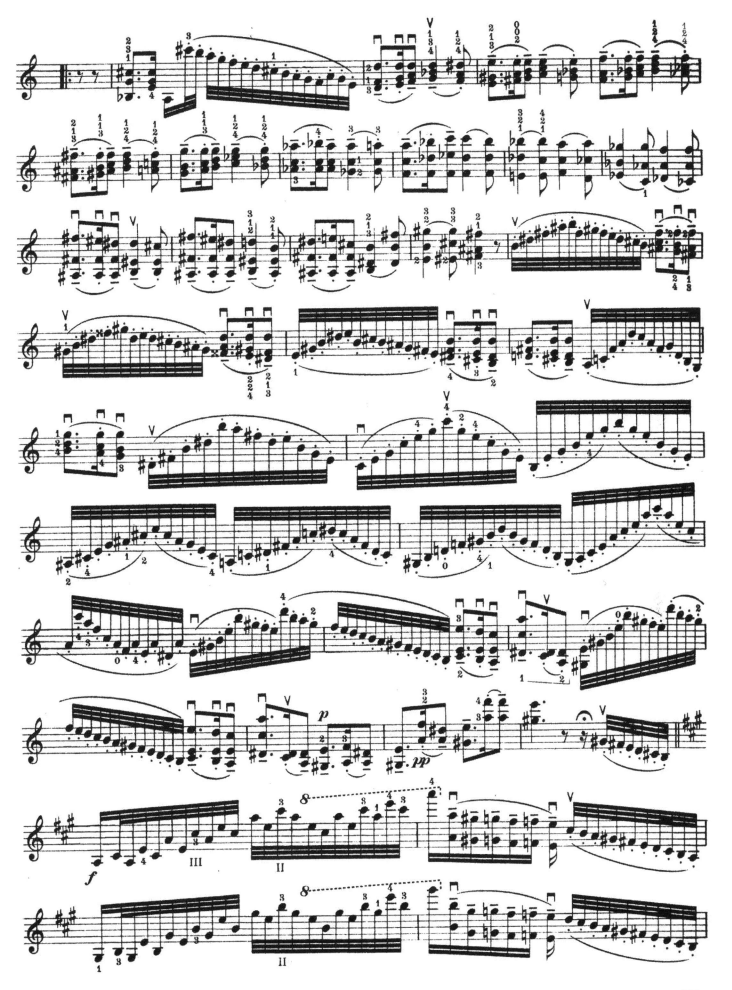

73

The double-stops with absolute clearness and faultless intonation.

76

The E major parts of this Caprice are played with light strokes at the lower third of the bow. The three-and four-part chords of the E minor parts are to be played with strength and decision, although the two staccato six-teenths are played with thrown staccato at the middle of the bow. The groups of five notes in the A minor part are also to be played with thrown staccato, although great care should be exercised that the tonal strength of the group played with the Up-stroke be absolutely the same as that of the Down-stroke group.

*) Near the fingerboard in imitation of two flutes.

**) In imitation of two French Horns (The fingers must be very firmly stopped while the bow moves lightly near the fin--ger-board.)

78

FLYING STACCATO. The bow, held with thumb and forefinger only, is thrown upon the string at a point about one quarter of its length from the tip. In order to produce this flying staccato with clear and absolutely distinct precision, the greatest care should be observed in string transfers. For detailed advice for mastering this variety of staccato bowing consult my Violin School (Virtuoso - Technics,) Book II.

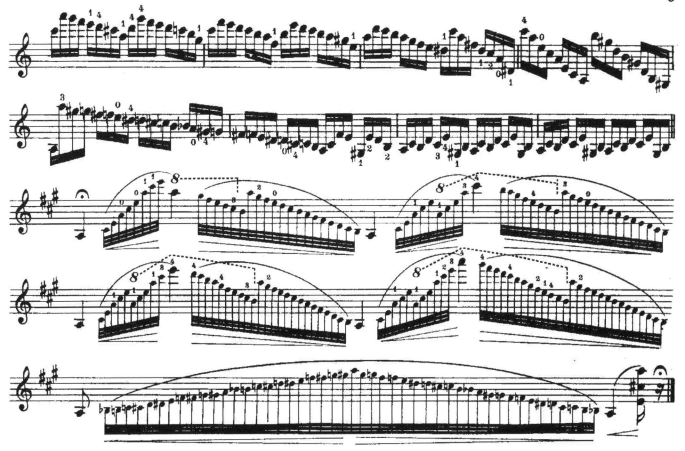

In order to produce the three-part chords to best-sounding advantage, the player should endeavor to obtain a firm hold upon the middle string with his bow. The pressure of the latter must always remain elastic in order that the beauty of tone may not be marred or destroyed. The *Presto* to be played with firm, clinging bow.

15522-52

81

83

84

85

The chromatic double-stops to be played with absolute clearness and faultless intonation. The detached sixteenths with the middle of the bow, lightly thrown.

*) Flying staccato with thrown bow as employed in the preceding Caprice, but covering a more extended range of notes.

90

With exception of the notes specially marked (*f*) this Caprice is to be played *mezza voce* throughout. Only so much of the middle of the bow to be used as is necessary to set the strings into vibration.

It is very difficult to produce the accented notes with the necessary precision and nicety, owing to the rapid tempo of this Caprice. This accentuation must never interfere in the slightest degree with the tempo at which the study is taken.

Not only must the various bowings be executed with the greatest rapidity but with absolute distinctness as well.

(For comparison, see my "Violin Method", Parts I and II and my edition of "Kreutzer's 42 Studies", revised in accordance with modern demands. Published by Carl Fischer, New York.)

No 1.
(No 16.)*)

*) The small figures in brackets indicate the numbering and order of succession in the original edition of these Caprices.

The chromatic scales in this Caprice to be played with utmost clearness and pearl-like perfection. For additional or preparatory matter of a like nature see my "Violin School", Part II, and my "Systematic Scale Studies, Book I and III, on the mastery of chromatic scales (Carl Fischer.)

To be practiced with both sets of fingering. Of these, the lower is preferable, as its use enables greater clearness and precision, besides avoiding continuous shifting of the fingers.

94

Use the bow at Middle, lightly thrown, for the passages in detached thirds. In regard to the *Allegro*, and for additional material of a similar nature, see my "Violin School," Part II and Book III of my "Systematic Scale Studies". (Carl Fischer, New York.)

D.C. La Corrente.

The last and first eighth of each bar with distinct and determined accent, although not roughly.

For preliminary or additional material for the G string passages see Part II of my Violin School and Book II of my "Systematic Scale Studies" (Scales on one string.) Carl Fischer, New York.

97

98

In the three-part chords of the following Caprice, the D string must be kept in constant vibration; to bring this about the middle string should be attacked with firmness and decision. The tone throughout must always be free, of beautiful quality, and never dull.

The melody in the *Amoroso* must be played with the utmost expressive feeling. In the *Presto* the flying staccato with thrown bow again demands careful attention. To be studied with both sets of fingering. Of the two, the lower fingering is preferable as its use enables greater clearness and precision besides avoid - ing continuous shifting of the fingers.

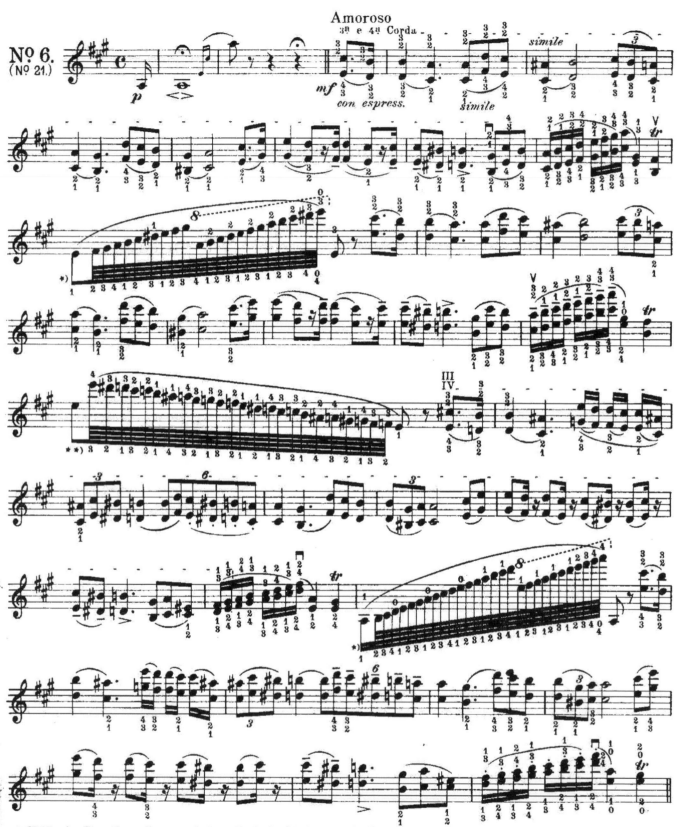

*) Shifts in Fourths. See my Systematic Scale Studies, Book II, as well as Preface to my edition of Kreutzer's Studies.
**)The lower fingering will enable clearer execution.

Presto.

In the *Minore* the flying staccato as described on page 8 (Caprice № 4) and the detached sixteenths in the middle of the bow with rebounding strokes.

As preparatory material for octave passages with the first and third fingers, such as are met with in the following Caprice, I would recommend the respective exercises in my Violin School (Book II) Part II and III, and my "Systematic Double Stop Studies" (Carl Fischer, New York)

D.C. al Fine

104

All notes marked ○ in the ninth Variation are played pizzicato with the left hand. For detailed information as to mastery of this particular variety of pizzicato playing see Part II of my Violin School.

VAR. 5

For additional suggestions about similar passages in double-stops compare my "Violin School," Part II and Book III of my "Systematic Scale Studies." (Carl Fischer, New York.)

VAR. 6

VAR. 7

For clear production of the three-part harmony in this variation, attack and hold the middle string firmly. In doing this the pressure of the bow must always remain elastic in order that the beauty of tone may not be marred or destroyed.

VAR. 8

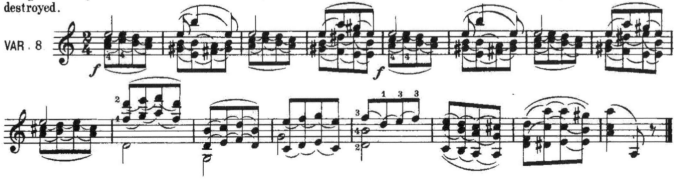

V Up-Bow. ⊙ Pizzicato: Pluck the string with the finger used for playing the previous note.

VAR. 9.

VAR. 10.

VAR. 11.

FINALE

Fine.

107

Forty-two Studies.

R. KREUTZER.

Adagio sostenuto.

108

This Étude may be practised with the same bowings as the preceding.
Allegro moderato.

The staccato must be practised very slowly to begin with, detaching all notes evenly with a loose wrist so that the bow does not quit the string. This is a sure way to learn this style of bowing well.

5. With broad stroke.

Allegro moderato.

This stroke must be executed firmly near the point of the bow, and all the notes must be perfectly e-ven in point of loudness, this evenness being attained by stronger pressure on the notes taken with up-bow, as these are naturally more difficult to emphasize than those with down-bow.

114

Bowing as in the preceding Étude.

Allegro assai.

7.

Allegro non troppo.

116

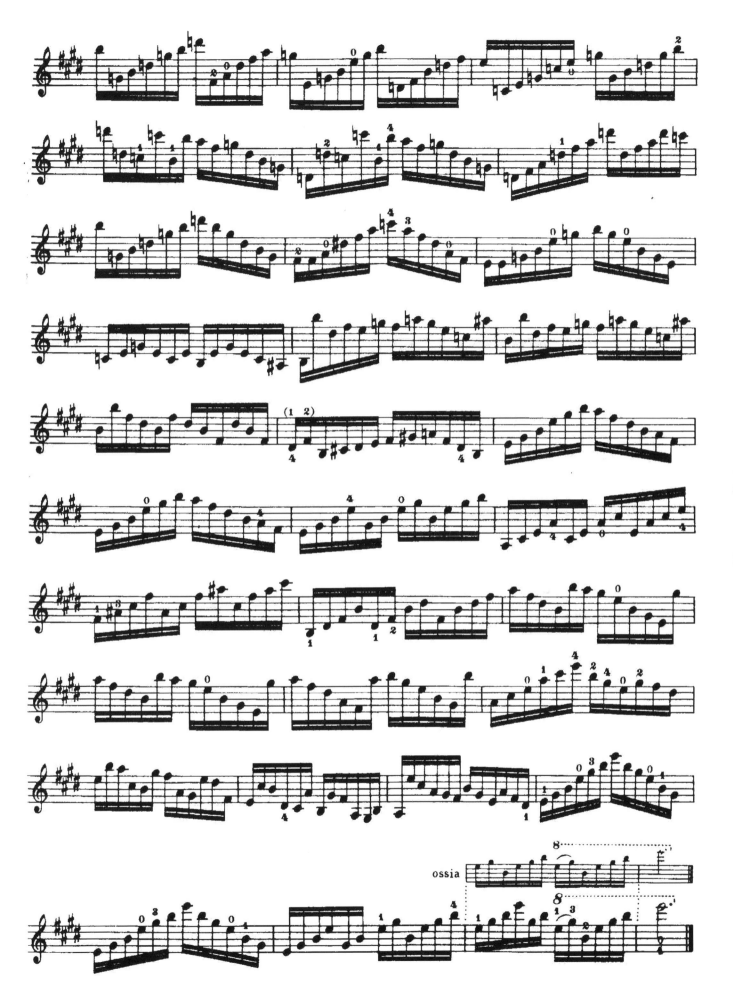

ossia

9. Allegro moderato.

119

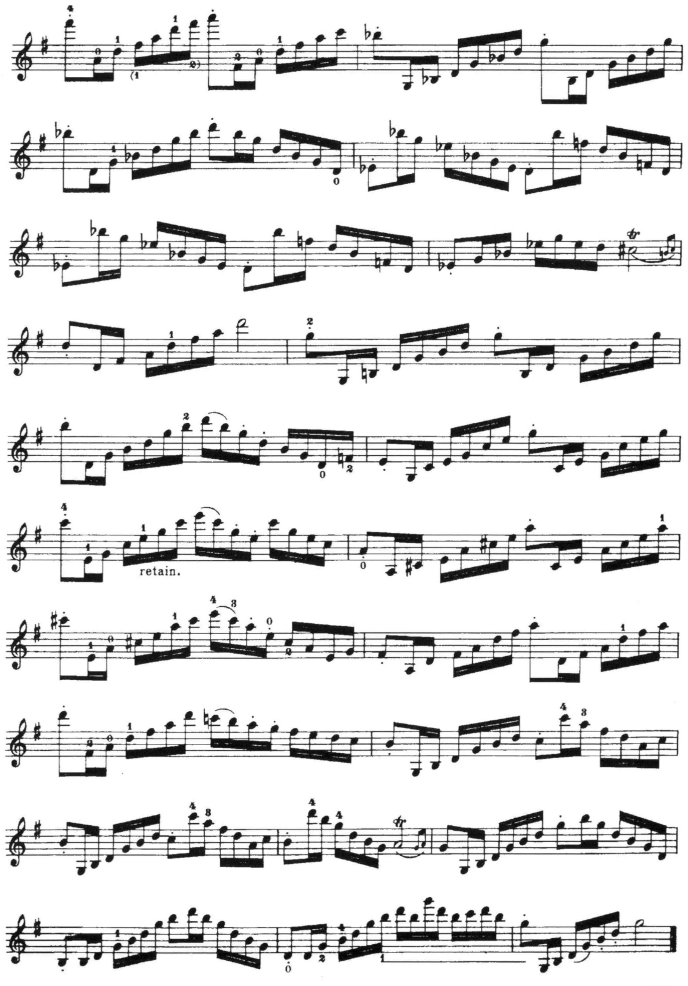

Andante.

Shift lightly and rapidly, so that no intermediate tones can be heard.

11.

122

12.

Moderato.
Keep the fingers down wherever possible.

124

125

14.

p

retain.

cresc.

cresc

p

IIª

retain.

p

128

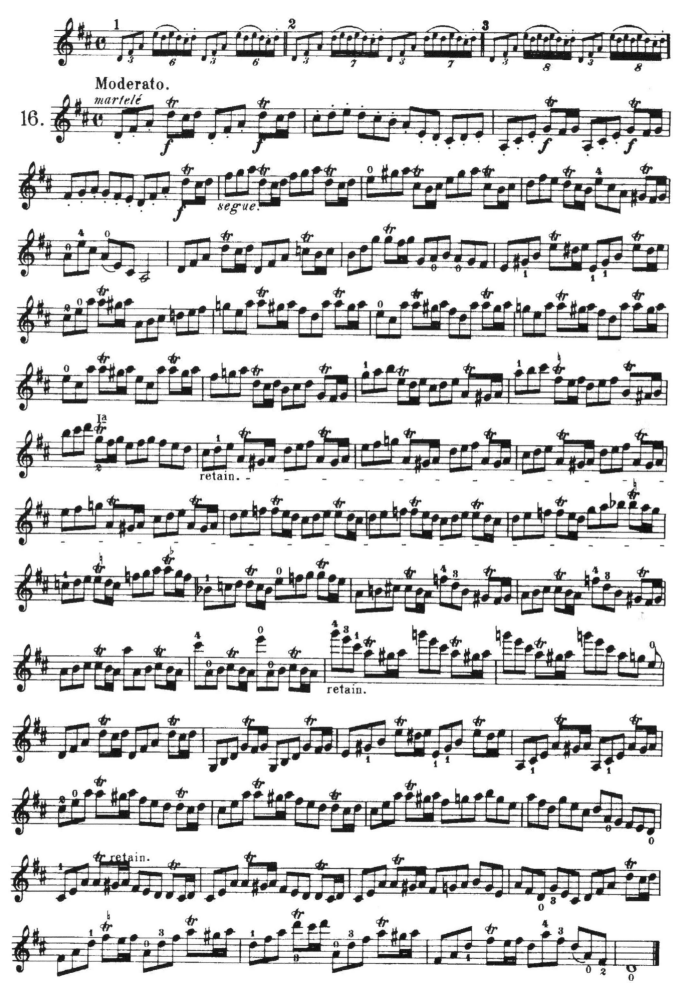

Moderato.

16.

131

retain

133

a) See Étude Nº 18, Note b.

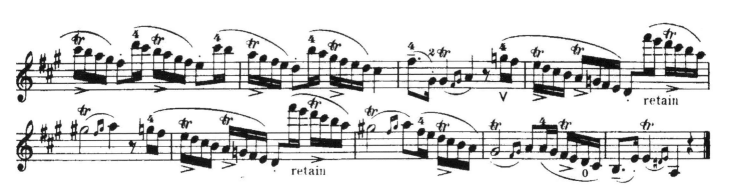

retain

retain

140

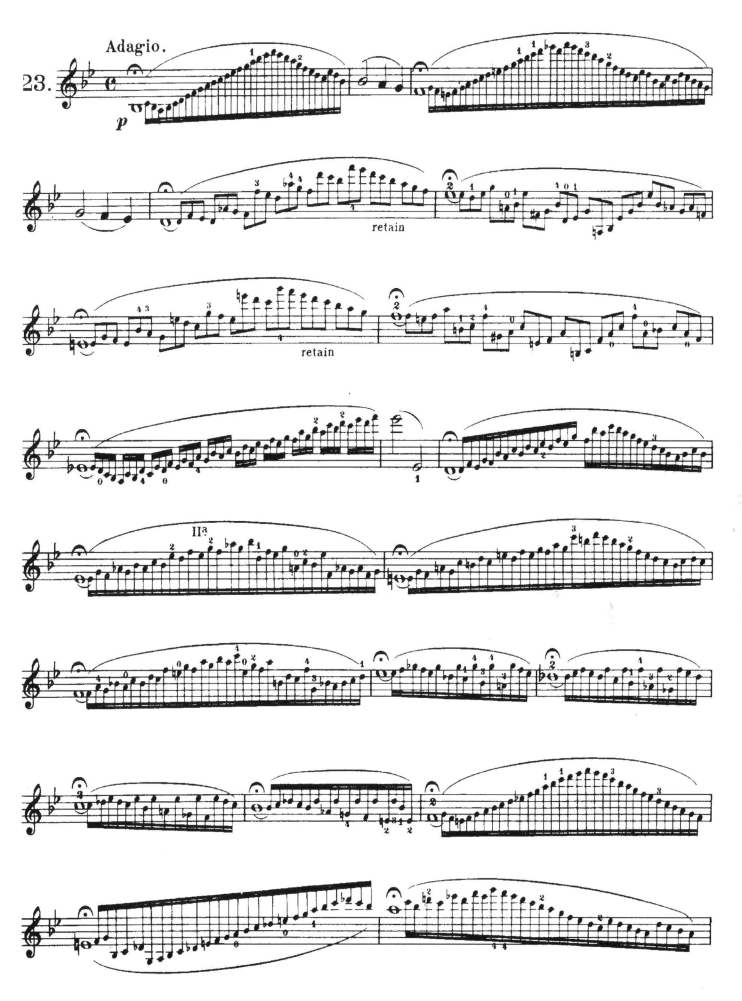

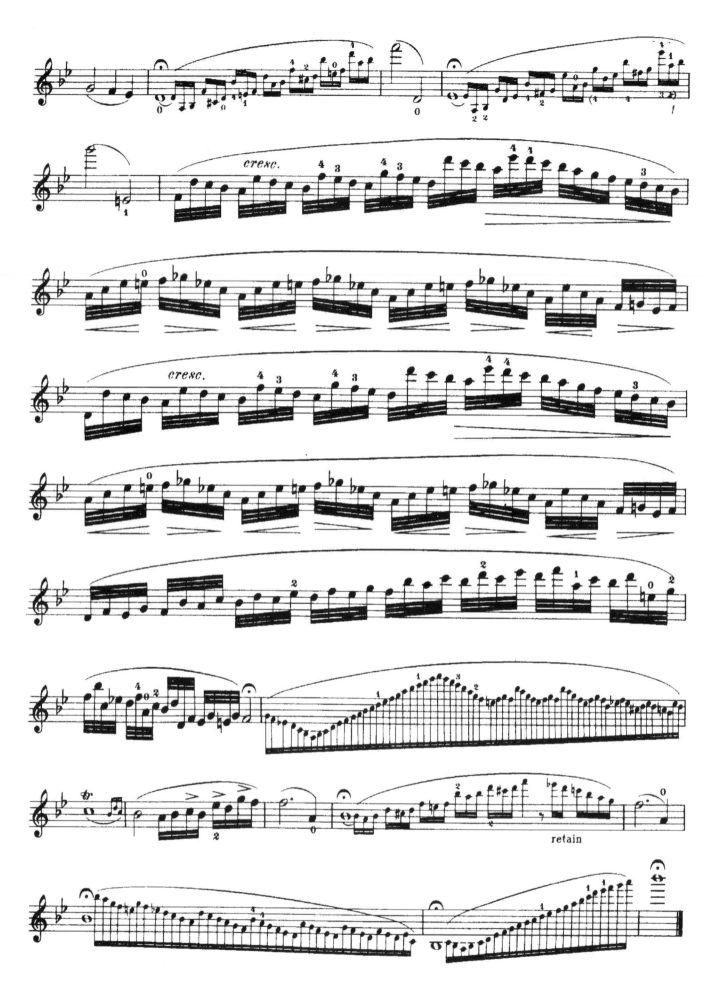

142

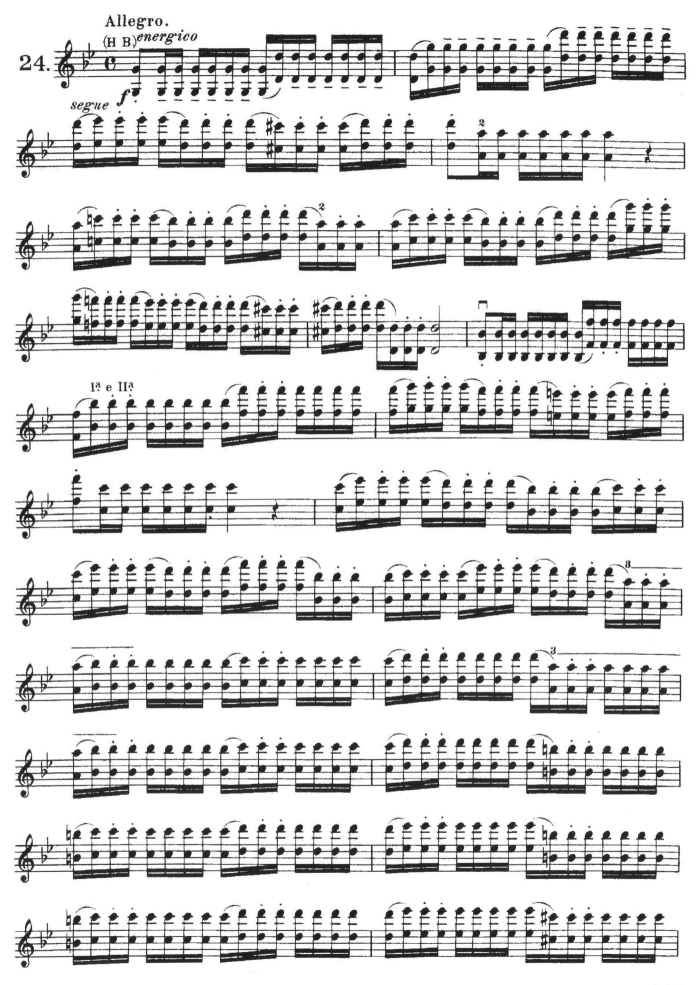

144

145

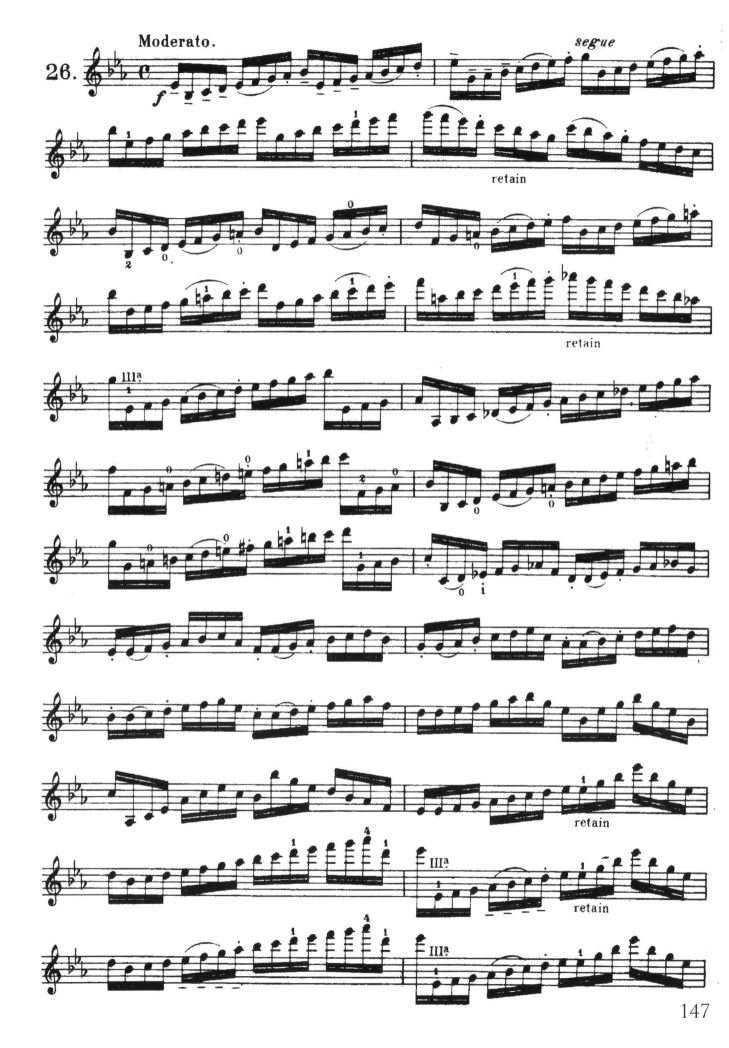

148

retain

150

28.

Grave.

ff

f

p   cre - - - - scen - - - - -

1a

a)

do - - - - - *f*

b)

sostenuto

p

p   *s*   *s*   *s*

retain

+) **Firm staccato at the point.**

a)   b)

152

Moderato. *Tranquilly and very evenly.*

29.

153

154

30. Moderato.

retain

Practise at first with 2 bows for each measure.

159

March.
Allegro maestoso.

35.

164

165

Allegro Vivace.

37.

segue.

retain.

167

168

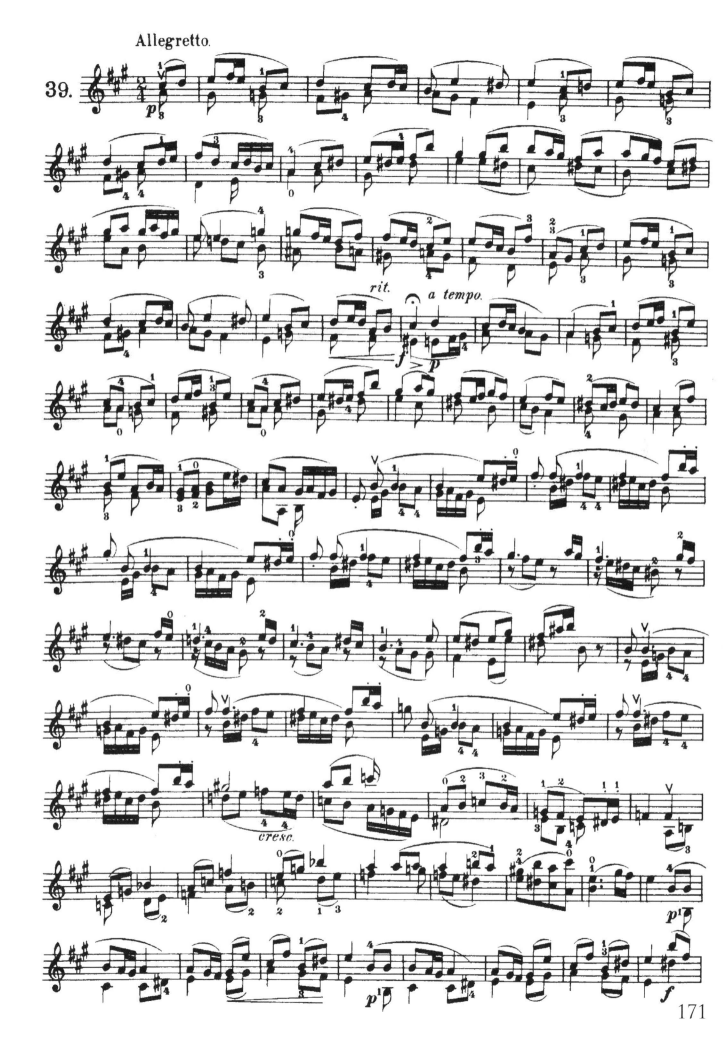

Allegretto.

39.

40.

173

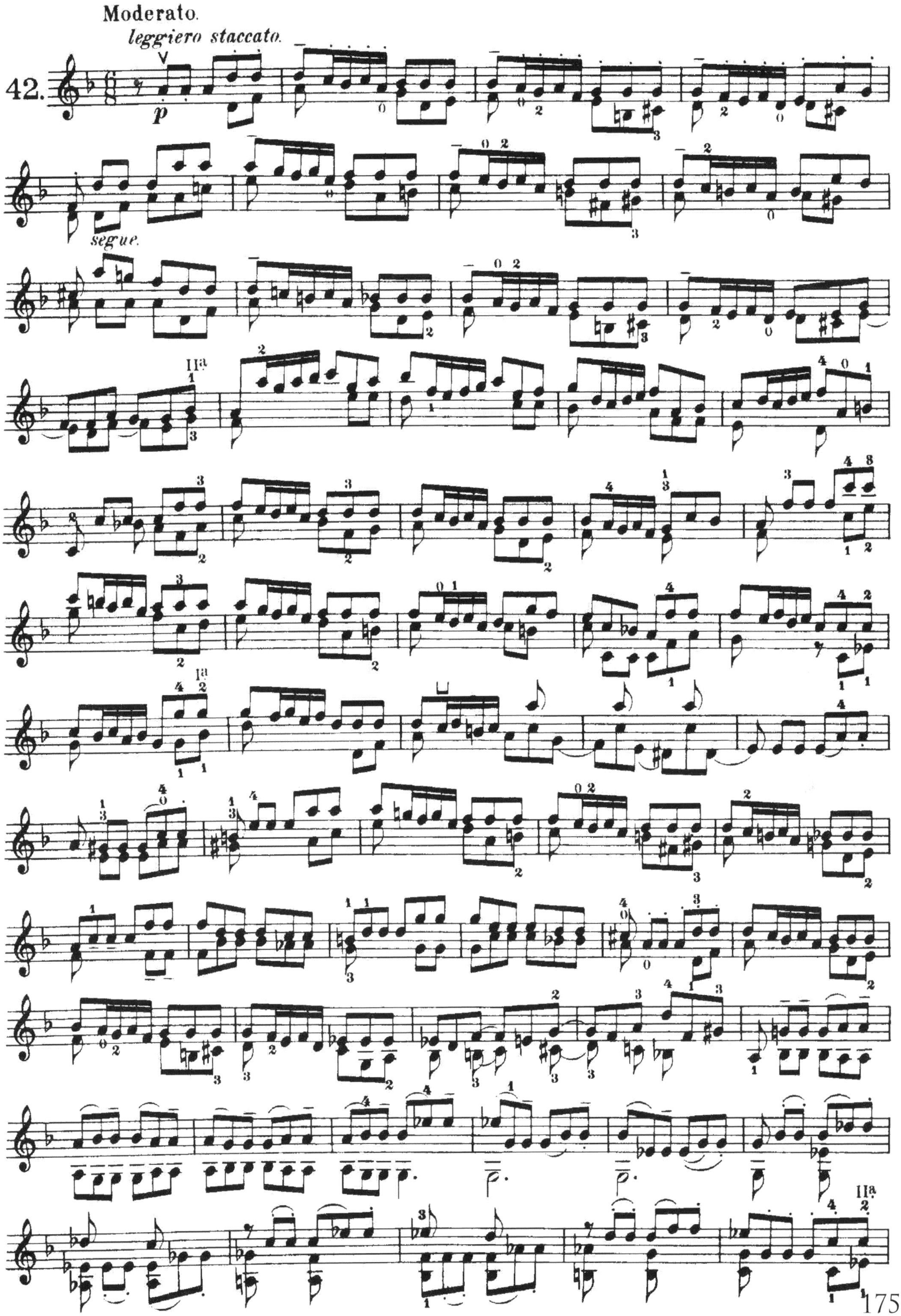
Moderato.
leggiero staccato.
42.
p
segue.
IIa

cre - - 2 - - scen - - - - -

- do - - - - f

al - - lar - - - gan - - - do.

This study should be played in the second position.

Commodo. (♩ = 120)

3.

dolce legato.

hold down 2nd finger.

181

Moderato. ($\bullet$ = 104)

5.

sempre marcato.

185

186

188

190

8. Moderato assai. ($\bullet$ = 100)

191

192

This study is to be played in the fourth position.

194

This study is to be played in the third position.

Allegretto. ($\flat$ = 96)

196

198

199

do not take too long bows.

201

Tempo I.

dolce.

un poco più mosso.

allargando.

203

204

207

f e sostenuto.

fz sostenuto.

Vivacissimo. (𝅗𝅥 = 132)

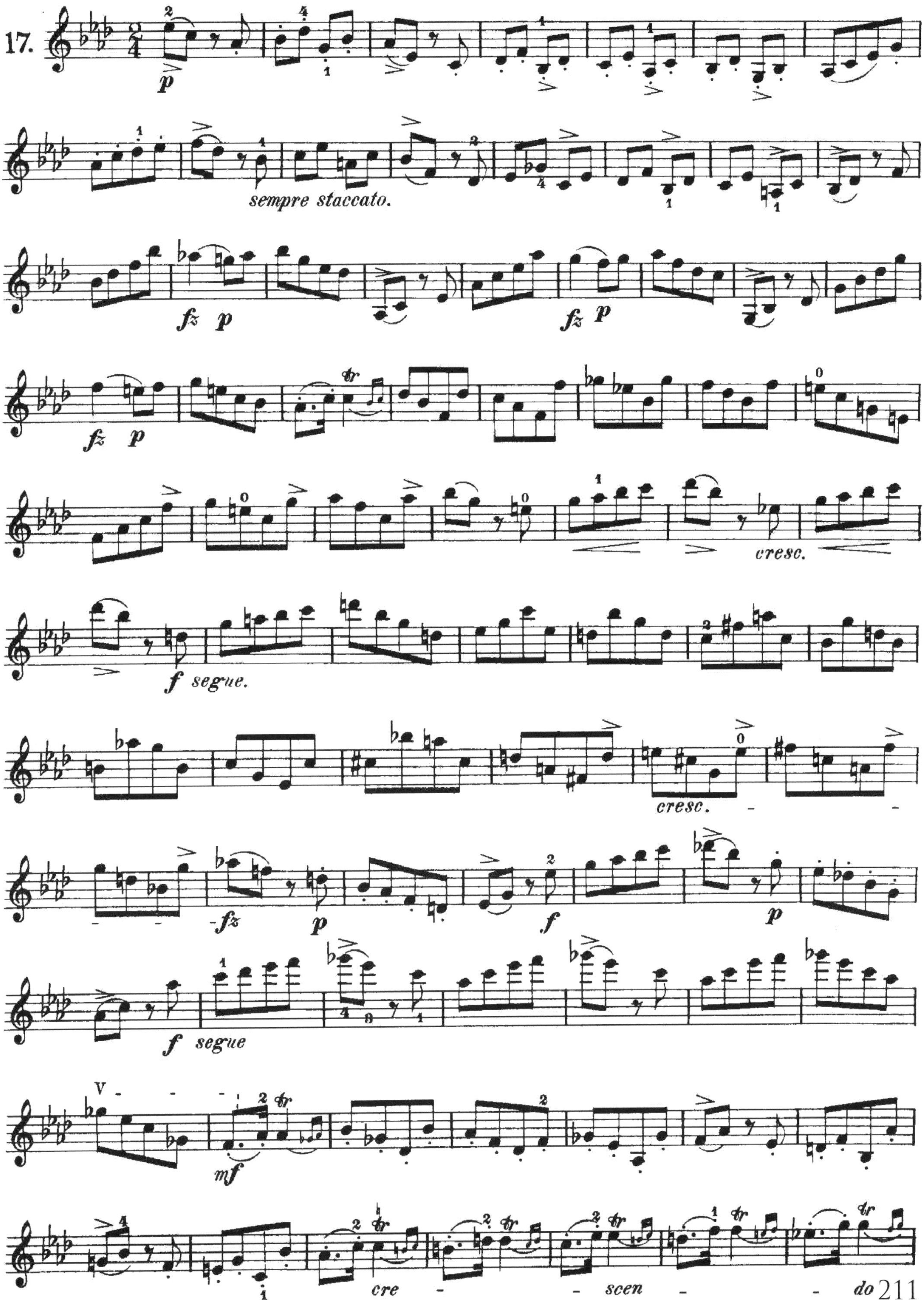

212

Arioso. ($\flat$ = 96)

19.

dolce.

attacca subito:

215

Allegretto.(♩.=84)

do not take too long bows.

hold down the third finger.

219

Presto. (♩. = 104)

22.

223

Moderato. ($\downarrow = 112$)

23.

f sostenuto.

224

225

227

PIETRO ROVELLI

PIETRO ROVELLI, one of the distinguished violinists of the first years of the nineteenth century, was the product of a number of diverse artistic influences. He came of a family of noted Italian musicians; he was the pupil of Rudolf Kreutzer, an artist formed in the school of the Stamitzes of Mannheim; he studied in Paris, and was considered to have modelled his style much on that of Viotti, the great Italian, so much of whose work was done in Paris. Pietro's father, Alessandro, was at one time conductor of the orchestra in Weimar. Another of the family, Giuseppe, was a violoncellist in the service of the court of Parma, where Pietro was born on February 6, 1793. His grandfather, Giovanni Battista Rovelli, was first violin of the orchestra of the church of Santa Maria Maggiore, at Bergamo. Pietro showed precocity of musical talent, which was promptly cultivated by his musical elders. He was put under the tuition of his grandfather, and by the time he was thirteen years old he was travelling as a prodigy through the cities of Italy and Switzerland and arousing widespread admiration. An influential music lover, the Senator Alessandri, was impressed by his promise, and sent him to study with the famous Rudolf Kreutzer in Paris, at that time first solo violinist at the Opéra and in the private band of Napoleon. There, too, the young Italian player won much admiration, and he was considered one of Kreutzer's best pupils. When his father, Alessandro, was appointed to the place in Weimar, the son followed him thither; but he soon set out again for Paris. When he reached Munich, however, he found his further progress blocked by the insistent admiration of that capital. He was promptly made "Royal Bavarian chamber musician" and first concerto player at the Bavarian court, and was loaded with rich gifts. He stayed several years in Munich, his fame increasing continually through the German cities in which he played. He gave a number of "Academies" or concerts of his own in Vienna, which were highly successful. While he was visiting the Austrian capital in 1817, he met and married Micheline, an accomplished piano player, daughter of Emmanuel Aloysius Foerster, at that time highly esteemed as a composer. Two years later Rovelli returned to his native city, Bergamo, where he was appointed first violinist of the church, the place his grandfather had held before him, and violin teacher in the music school. But teaching was not to his taste, and he confined himself thereafter to playing solos. He suffered much from bad health, and died on September 8, 1838.

Rovelli's playing was considered "simple, expressive, graceful, noble; on the whole, classical; the kind of playing that wins the heart of the listener." Such was the judgment of the *Allgemeine musikalische Zeitung* after his death. Rovelli had at least two noted pupils, Molique and Täglichsbeck, both of whom studied with him during his sojourn in Munich. He left a considerable number of compositions that are still highly esteemed by violinists, especially his Caprices; he also wrote several concertos and string quartets.

RICHARD ALDRICH.

Twelve Caprices.

□ Down - bow
V Up - bow

I: E - string.
II: A - string.
III: D - string.
IV: G - string.

Violin.

PIETRO ROVELLI.

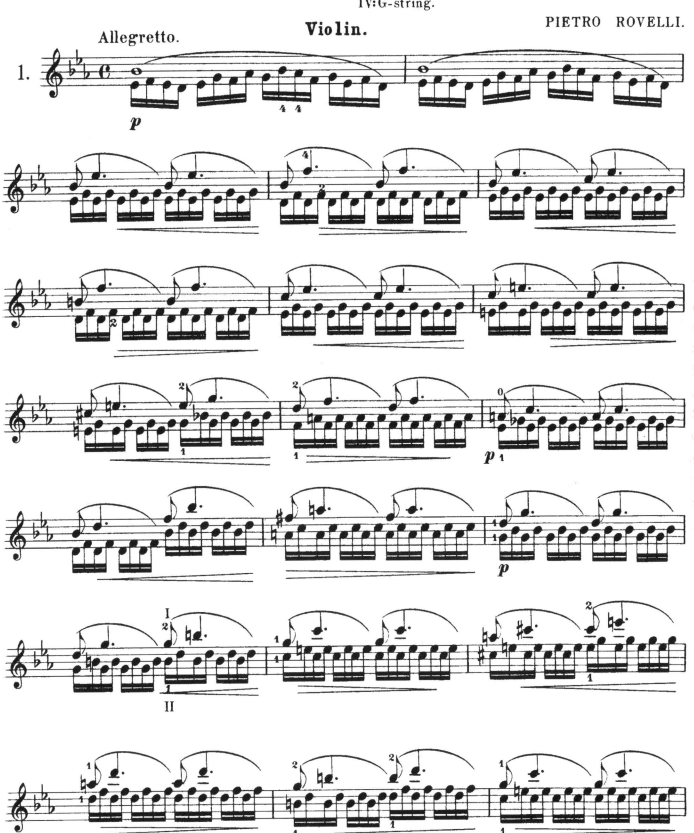

Note: The fingers should not be lifted from the strings unnecessarily. The first finger in particular should be kept on the string as much as possible.

229

230

Note: The finger employed in stopping the upper note should not be lifted until necessary.

233

235

236

237

239

240

243

244

245

248

250

251

252

253

Concerto for Two Violins

Violin I

J. S. Bach

255

256

Largo, ma non tanto
(The theme is to be played with a full, soft tone)

257

Concerto for Two Violins

Violin II

J. S. Bach

Largo, ma non tanto

(The theme is to be played with a full, soft tone)

264

265

Perpetuum Mobile.
(Perpetual Motion.)

The notes, individually considered, must be played with utmost evenness and equality, at middle of bow, with hair slightly tighter than usual and in Spiccato manner. With exception of the prescribed dynamics, the composition should be played *Mezzo-forte* throughout. To be practiced at first with aid of a metronome.

This composition is particularly well adapted for public performance. (The most effective and best arranged piano accompaniment part is published by Carl Fischer, New York.)

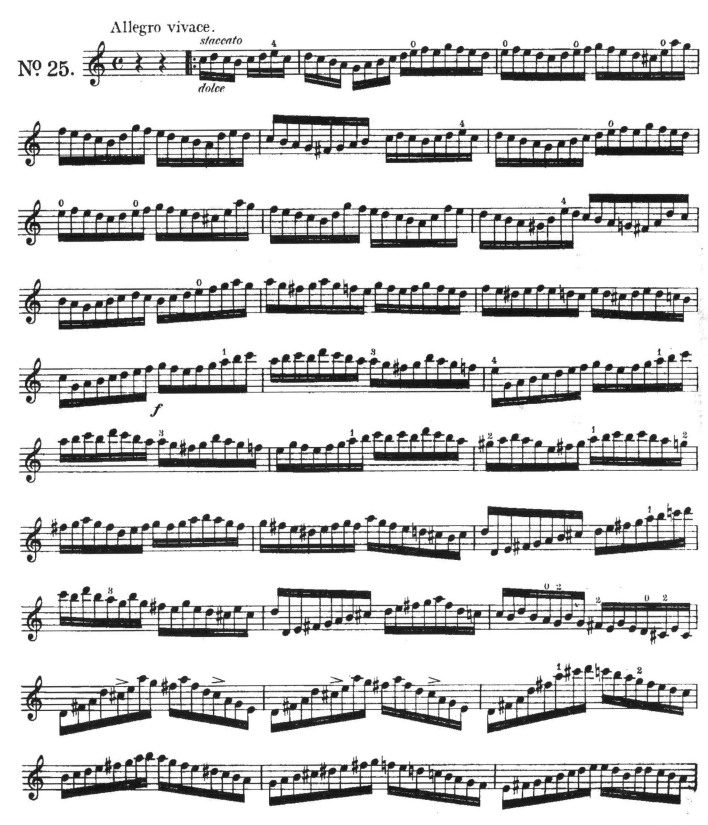

270

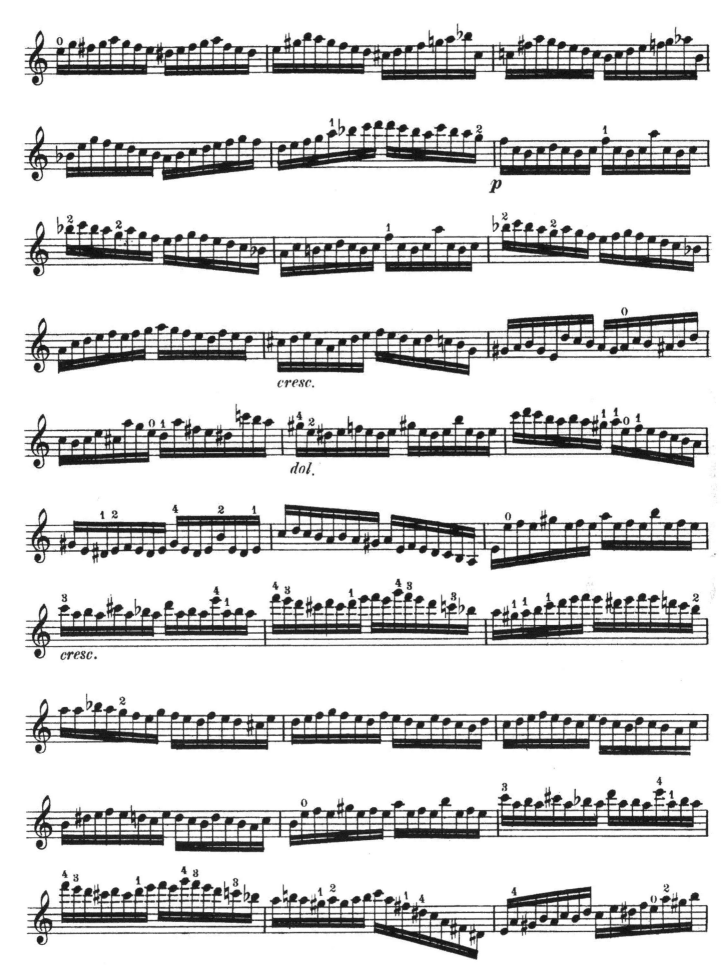

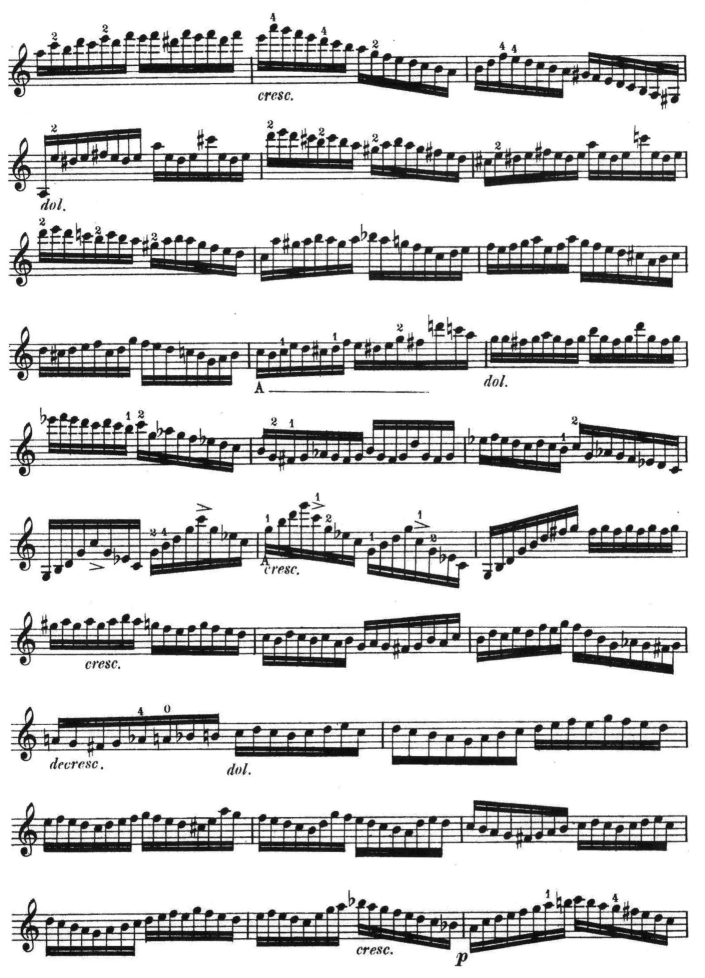

272

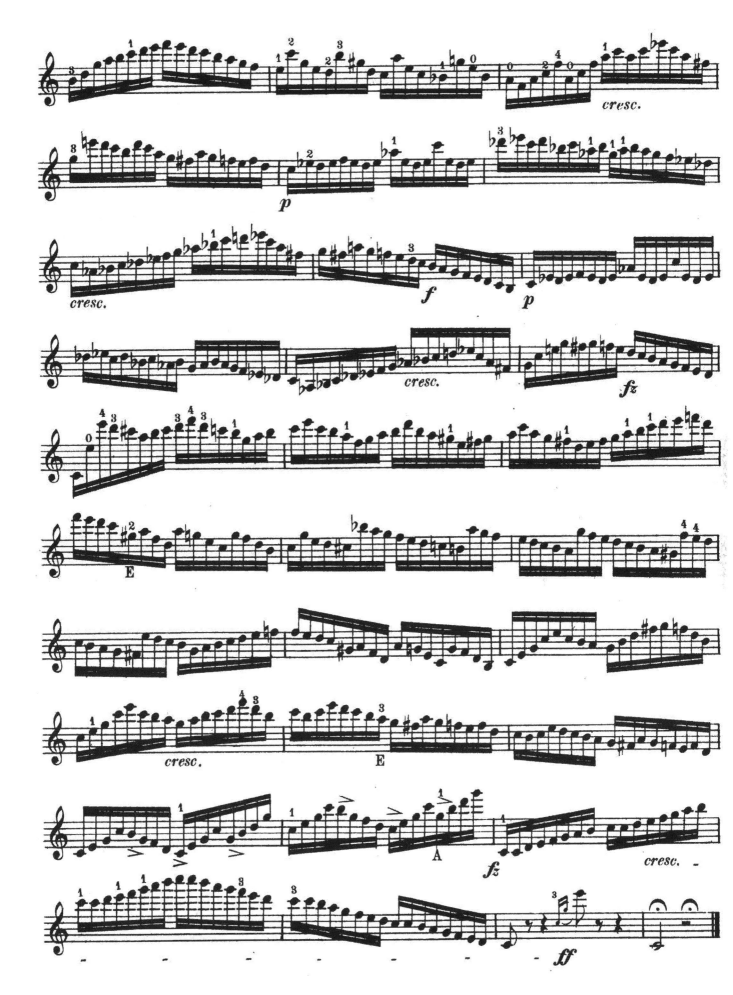

Duo.

DUET FOR ONE VIOLIN.

This duet for one violin, also excellently adapted for public performance, is exceptionally difficult owing to its pizzicato accompaniment to the melody. If well performed, it should sound as though played by two violins.

Part II of my Violin School contains special exercises for this particular technical difficulty and use of same as preparatory material for this Duo will be found very beneficial.

*) 3P, 4 P, indicates: The pizzicato is played with the 3d or 4th finger.

SONATA.

Op. 12, Nº 1.

VIOLIN.

Allegro con brio.

L. van Beethoven.

Tema con Variazioni.
Andante con moto.

Var. I.

Var. II.

280

279

281

fin

Made in the USA
San Bernardino, CA
13 December 2013